Think Like the Rich, Earn Like the Rich
Handbook for Wealth

Table of Contents

introduction

1.1 Welcome to the World of Wealth

In the shadows of daily routine and perceived limitations, lies a secret realm waiting to be discovered: the exciting world of wealth. Imagine a universe where opportunities flash like stars in the night, where dreams become shiny coins that fall from the sky. This is the place where bold minds and brave hearts bring their aspirations to life.

Welcome to the odyssey of wealth, where every step is a dance between your wildest dreams and tangible reality. This manual is not just a book; It is a portal to a domain where bold thinking meets determined action. Prepare to explore the depths of your own mind, challenging conventions and embracing a fundamental truth: wealth is not just a financial state; It is a state of mind.

Here, in this corner of the literary universe, we will enter together into the jungle of opportunities, we will trace the secret paths of the millionaire mentality and we will learn to dance under the moon of abundance. You are the hero of this story, and every word you find will be a compass on your journey to prosperity.

As you immerse yourself in these pages, let welcoming the world of wealth be the threshold you cross with determination and curiosity. The path is yours to explore, and the riches wait to be unearthed. Are you ready to challenge your destiny and forge a path to abundance?

With our eyes set on the horizon of infinite possibilities, let's begin this exciting journey towards a life where thinking like the rich will guide you to earning like the rich. Go forth, brave explorer, the world of wealth awaits your arrival!

1.2 Importance of the Millionaire Mentality

Under the canopy of stars weaving stories in the vast sky of possibility, we now dive into the mysteries of the millionaire mentality. In this chapter, we will discover that the true treasure is not always found in the coffers, but in the winding paths of the mind.

In the forest of thoughts, the millionaire mentality emerges like the river that gives life to the jungle of your dreams. Imagine, for a moment, that every thought is a dancing leaf on the breeze of opportunity, and that cultivating the right mindset is like watering the roots of your own tree of prosperity.

From the hills of doubt to the valleys of conviction, we explore how the great architects of wealth shape their mental foundations. The importance of the millionaire mentality lies not only in accumulating material wealth, but in building an inner palace resistant to the storms of life.

Here, in this literary corner, we will learn to tune in to our thoughts, to tune into the frequency of abundance. The millionaire mentality is not just a set of beliefs; It is a spell that transforms obstacles into opportunities and doubts into fuel for success.

Every word you find on these pages is a brush on the canvas of your mindset. So, brave explorer, dive into the stream of possibility and let the importance of the millionaire mindset be the melody that guides your steps.

In the next tour of this journey, you will discover how your thoughts have the power to sculpt your destiny, how the millionaire mentality will make you the architect of your own fortune. Go ahead, intrepid seeker of secrets, the universe of wealth awaits your reflections!

II. Fundamentals of the Millionaire Mentality

Under the silver light of the moon, we venture beyond the thickets of everyday thinking and explore the Fundamentals of the Millionaire Mindset. In this chapter, we will discover the cornerstones that support the temple of mental wealth, where each foundation is a footprint on the path to opulence.

2.1 Beliefs that Bring You Closer to Wealth

In the clearing of convictions, we meet the magical creatures of self-belief and trust in unlimited potential. We learn that beliefs are not just words; They are spells that weave the tapestry of your reality.

Discover how the beliefs you hold dear to your heart are the seeds that bloom in fields of opportunity.

2.2 Breaking Mental Barriers

The meandering path of the millionaire mindset is often hindered by invisible barriers. Here, among the shadows and the flashes of fireflies, we will learn to break the chains of self-limitation. Each step is a declaration of independence, each act of bravery is a blow against the walls that separate dreams from reality.

2.3 Visualization and Financial Positivism

In the magical clearing of visualization, we discover the art of painting with light the reality we desire. Dreams become more tangible, desires become star maps to success. In this corner of the literary forest, we explore how financial positivity is the light that guides your steps in the darkness, transforming visions into achievements.

Each word written here is a spell, each paragraph a poetry that invites you to unravel the secrets of the millionaire mentality. So, brave explorers, step into the mists of belief, challenge mental barriers and let visualization be your flashlight on the path to wealth.

In the next chapter, we dive even deeper into the depths of the mind, where we will discover the thinking strategies that fuel the growth of

inner fortune.

III. Millionaire Thinking Strategies

Among the dancing shadows of thoughts, we immerse ourselves in the enchanted waters of Millionaire Thinking Strategies. Here, each strategy is a flash of light that illuminates the path to inner greatness.

3.1 Adopting Successful Habits

In the clearing of transformation, we discover how habits are the roots that support the tree of prosperity. Each repeated act is a note in the symphony of success. We explore the daily rituals that weave the fabric of wealth and how adopting successful habits is like sowing seeds that will grow in the garden of your destiny.

3.2 The Importance of Self-Confidence

In the forest of self-exploration, we encounter the magical creature of self-confidence. We discovered that self-confidence is the mirror that reflects your infinite potential.

Learn how nurturing this essential gift allows you to navigate challenges and embrace every opportunity with courage.

3.3 Overcoming the Fear of Failure

Under the mantle of the constellation of courage, we face the fear of failure. Here, among the fireflies that flicker in the darkness of uncertainty, we explore how failure is not an end, but rather another chapter in the epic of wealth.

Discover how to overcome the fear of failure and spread your wings to new heights.

Each page is a path in this forest of millionaire thinking strategies, where each tip is an arrow pointing to the top of the mountain of prosperity.

So, brave explorers, enter the jungle of transformation, embrace self-confidence and let courage dissolve the fear of failure.

In the next chapter, we will explain the opportunities that await at the confluence of bold thinking and determined action. Go ahead, intrepid visionary, the world of wealth awaits

your firm steps!

IV. Building your Wealth from Home

Under the shining moon of opportunities, we venture into the chapter of "Building Your Wealth from Home". Here, you will discover that your home is not only the refuge of your dreams, but also the quarry from which you will carve your fortune.

4.1 Online Income Opportunities

In the digital village of opportunity, we explore how the vast plains of the network offer fertile fields to sow the seeds of prosperity. Learn how to identify online income opportunities, where each click is one more step towards creating wealth from the comfort of your home.

4.2 Entrepreneurship from Home

At the top of the hill of entrepreneurship, we find the strength of those who turn their passions into thriving businesses.

Discover how starting a business from home is not only an act of courage, but also a journey towards financial autonomy. Here, each dream is a seed that germinates in the garden of your own business.

4.3 Remote Work and Financial Freedom

Under the canopy of nomadic skies, we explore how remote work becomes the

rainbow that connects your skills
with global opportunities.

Discover how financial freedom is
intertwined with the flexibility of
remote work, where each task
completed is one more step towards
achieving your goals.
In this chapter, each word is a flash
of light on the path to building your
wealth from home.

So, brave dream builder, enter the
workshop of digital opportunity,
start from home and let financial
freedom be your guide on this journey
towards abundance.
At the next bend in this literary
forest, we explore financial planning
as a star map that will lead you to
the treasure of prosperity.

Go forth, intrepid architect of your
destiny, the kingdom of wealth awaits

your creativity!

V. Financial Planning for Success

Into the moonlit glade of financial wisdom, we step into the chapter "Financial Planning for Success." Here, you'll learn how to chart your own star map, charting your course toward the promised land of financial freedom.

5.1 Defining Financial Goals

In the garden of goals, we discover that each dream is a seed that grows with proper care. Learn how defining clear financial goals is like laying the foundation for your own fortune. Each goal is a star that guides your steps towards the firmament of prosperity.

5.2 Budget and Expense Control

On the path of financial control, we find the magic tool of the budget. Discover how every coin spent is a decision that defines your journey to wealth. We explore how spending control is not a restriction, but a key that opens the doors to a balanced financial life.

5.3 Smart Investments

Under the rainbow of investment opportunities, we explore how to make every penny work for you. Discover how smart investments are not just transactions, but collaborators on your journey to wealth creation. Each investment decision is one more step towards building your financial empire.

Every word written in this chapter is a jewel in the chest of financial wisdom.

So, brave financial navigator, enter the sea of goals, master the waves of budgeting and let smart investments be your compass on this journey to prosperity.

In the next chapter, we dive into the entrepreneurial mindset and discover how entrepreneurship can be the key to unlocking the doors to the realm of wealth. Go ahead, intrepid financial planner, the universe of abundance awaits your wise decisions!

VI. Developing an Entrepreneurial Mindset

Under the starry vault of creativity and innovation, we immerse ourselves in the chapter "Developing an Entrepreneurial Mindset". Here, you will discover how each idea is a seed that can bloom in the garden of business success.

6.1 Entrepreneurship and Wealth

In the meadow of possibility, we meet the architects of dreams who turn ideas into realities. Discover how entrepreneurship is not only an act of creating businesses, but also of forging your own path to wealth.

Every project is an opportunity for growth and prosperity.

6.2 Creation and Management of Successful Businesses

In the creation workshop, we explore how every successful business is a testament to vision and dedication. Learn how efficient business management is like conducting an orchestra, where each element contributes to the symphony of success. Each strategy is a note that will resonate at the heart of your financial empire.

6.3 Networking and Strategic Alliances

In the relationship market, we delve into the importance of networking and strategic alliances. Discover how every connection is a bridge that brings you closer to unexplored opportunities.

We explore how building a strong network and forming strategic alliances can be the compass that guides your journey to business success.

Every word written in this chapter is a flash of inspiration on the path to developing an entrepreneurial mindset. So, brave empire builder, delve into the forging of ideas, masterfully direct your business orchestra and let connections and alliances be the pillars of your fortune.

In the next chapter, we will explain how to overcome obstacles and challenges, learning that failure is not a defeat, but a lesson on the

path to wealth.

VII. Overcoming Obstacles and Challenges

Under the starry sky of resilience and perseverance, we immerse ourselves in the chapter "Overcoming Obstacles and Challenges". Here, you will discover that every adversity is an opportunity in disguise, and every challenge is a test that will strengthen your journey to wealth.

7.1 Learning from Failures

In the valley of lessons, we encounter the tumultuous rivers of failures. Discover how every setback is a learning opportunity, and every mistake is a springboard to success.

We will learn to embrace failures as fellow travelers, understanding that temporary defeat is the precursor to final victory.

7.2 Resilience and Persistence

Under the canopy of resilient trees, we explore resilience and persistence as the magical tools that allow you to weather the storms.

Learn how every blow is an opportunity to get stronger, and every challenge is an invitation to prove your bravery.

Resilience and persistence are your allies on the journey to the top.

7.3 Financial Crisis Management

In the embrace of the financial storm, we discover how crisis management is a fundamental skill.

Learn how to turn uncertainty into opportunity, and how each crisis is a crossroads that offers you the possibility of reinventing yourself.

In this chapter, we explore strategies for facing crises with intelligence and determination.

Every word written in this chapter is a drop of wisdom that will help you navigate the turbulent waters of financial life.

So, brave warriors of fortune, enter the battlefield with your head held high, learn from failures, cultivate resilience and master the art of overcoming challenges.

In the next chapter, we will unravel the keys to becoming a millionaire, revealing practical strategies to increase income, multiply your wealth, and adopt a philosophy of abundance. Go forth, fearless achiever, the universe of wealth awaits your master moves!

VIII. Keys to Becoming a Millionaire

Under the constellation of abundance, we enter the chapter "Keys to Becoming a Millionaire." Here, you will discover that wealth is not just a destination, but an ongoing journey, and that every action is a key that unlocks new doors to opulence.

8.1 Strategies to Increase Income

In the field of unexplored opportunities, we explore practical strategies to increase income. Discover how every focused effort is an investment in your own potential. Learn to identify and capitalize on opportunities that bring you closer to the threshold of wealth.

8.2 Multiplying your Heritage

Under the radiant sun of multiplication, we delve into how to make your wealth grow exponentially. Explore investment strategies, smart savings, and multiplying resources to build a solid financial empire. Every financial decision is a stone in the building of your fortune.

8.3 Philosophy of Abundance

At the top of the mountain of reflection, we immerse ourselves in the philosophy of abundance. Discover how every thought of gratitude and generosity is a seed that blooms in the garden of wealth. Learn to adopt an abundance mindset that will transform not only your financial situation, but your perception of the world.

Every word in this chapter is a key that opens doors to financial mastery and personal fulfillment.

So, brave architect of your destiny, delve into the treasure of strategies, multiply your wealth and let the philosophy of abundance be the guide of your journey to the financial summit.

In the next section, we will explain how to live a life of wealth and meaning, understanding that prosperity not only is measured in financial terms, but in the fullness of human experience.

Forward, intrepid seeker of true wealth, the kingdom of abundance

awaits your conscious steps!

IX. Living a Life of Wealth and Meaning

In the garden of plenitude, we enter the chapter "Living a Life of Wealth and Meaning." Here, you will discover that true wealth is not only measured in numbers, but in meaningful experiences that give meaning to your journey through life.

9.1 Social Impact and Philanthropy

In the corner illuminated by the glow of compassion, we explore social impact and philanthropy as fundamental aspects of wealth. Discover how each act of generosity is an investment in collective well-being. Learn to weave a network of social support and contribute to the flourishing of entire communities.

9.2 Work-Life Balance

At the crossroads between the sun of work and the moon of personal life, we delve into the importance of balance. We explore how every moment spent at work should be balanced with time for self-care, relationships, and personal exploration. Learn how to build a fulfilling life that not only accumulates wealth, but also celebrates the richness of existence.

9.3 Enjoying Wealth with Purpose

Under the constellation of personal fulfillment, we discover the importance of enjoying wealth with purpose. Explore how every financial achievement can be a means to achieving deeper goals and contributing to the well-being of the world.

Learn to infuse each day with a purpose that transcends the material.

Every word in this chapter is a guide that will take you beyond the simple accumulation of wealth to a life full of meaning.

So, brave navigators of existence, enter the ocean of social impact, seek work-life balance, and let enjoying wealth with purpose be the compass of your journey.

In the final conclusion, we recap the key teachings of this journey and outline the next steps on your path to wealth and personal fulfillment.

Go ahead, intrepid architect of your destiny, the universe of plenitude awaits your conscious decisions!

X. Conclusion

At the top of the mountain of financial wisdom, we come to the final chapter, the "Conclusion." Here, we recap the lessons learned and chart the next steps on your exciting journey to wealth and personal fulfillment.

10.1 Recapitulation of Main Teachings

In the mirror of hindsight, we reflect on the lessons you have explored throughout this journey. From the importance of the millionaire mindset to strategies for building wealth from home, each chapter has been a stepping stone on the path to financial mastery.

10.2 Your Journey Towards Wealth

With your backpack loaded with wisdom, we invite you to contemplate the next steps on your journey. What are your financial goals? How to integrate the philosophy of abundance into your daily life? This is your time to chart your own path to wealth and personal fulfillment.

Remember, this book is not just a guide, but a traveling companion in your quest for abundance. Wealth is not just about accumulating coins, but also about harvesting meaningful experiences and contributing to the well-being of those around you.

With every page you've explored, you've unearthed gems of knowledge that empower you on your journey. So, brave seekers of wealth, we urge you to move forward with determination, to embrace opportunities with boldness, and to build a life that reflects the fullness of your dreams.

May your journey to wealth be as vast and fascinating as the universe itself! With gratitude and optimism, I wish you success in every step you take.

End of "Think Like the Rich, Earn Like the Rich: A Handbook for Wealth." May your days be filled with prosperity and meaning!